Lions
Are
Awesome!

by Lisa J. Amstutz

Consultant: Jackie Gai, DVM
Captive Wildlife Vet

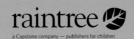

raintree

a Capstone company — publishers for children

Raintree is an imprint of Capstone Global Library Limited, a company incorporated in England and Wales having its registered office at 7 Pilgrim Street, London, EC4V 6LB – Registered company number: 6695582

www.raintree.co.uk
myorders@raintree.co.uk

Edited by Mari Bolte and Erika Shores
Designed by Cynthia Della-Rovere
Picture research by Svetlana Zhurkin
Production by Morgan Walters
Printed and bound in China by Nordica.
0914/CA21401520

ISBN 978-1-406-28847-6
18 17 16 15 14
10 9 8 7 6 5 4 3 2 1

British Library Cataloguing in Publication Data
A full catalogue record for this book is available from the British Library.

Acknowledgements
Dreamstime: Robin Van Olderen, 12, SandraRBarba, 6—7, Smellme, 16 (right); Newscom: ZUMA Press/Tony Crocetta, 26—27; Shutterstock: Aaron Amat, 27 (top), ala737, 13 (bottom), Alta Oosthuizen, 15 (top), 18, Ana Gram, 25, 29 (inset), bjogroet, 11 (top), Black Sheep Media (grass), throughout, Chantal de Bruijne (African landscape), back cover and throughout, creative, 10, e2dan, 13 (top), Eric Isselee, cover, back cover, 1, 4, 7 (top), 11 (bottom), 21 (top), 23 (top), 32, Gerrit_de_Vries, 14 (top), 17, Jez Bennett, 14 (bottom), John Michael Evan Potter, 9, Maggy Meyer, 28—29, MattiaATH, 8, Mogens Trolle, 15 (bottom), moizhusein, 20—21, 23, Moments by Mullineux, 5, Sean Stanton, 19, Serge Vero, 24, Stuart G. Porter, 22

We would like to thank Jackie Gai, DVM, for her invaluable help in the preparation of this book.

Contents

Amazing cats

Roar! The sound echoes across the plains. A lion's roar can be heard 8 kilometres (5 miles) away.

Lions are among the world's biggest cats. Males grow to about 2.4 metres (8 feet) long. They can measure up to 1.2 metres (4 feet) tall at the shoulder. Female lions are slightly smaller.

A lion's fur is golden in colour. It matches the dry grass of its African habitat. This helps to hide the lion from its prey.

6

Male lions grow a long, shaggy mane. A mane makes them look bigger. It can also protect them in fights. Manes grow darker each year.

Most lions live in central and southern Africa.
They roam open woodlands and grassy plains.
About 400 lions live in the Gir Forest of India.
These lions are in danger of dying out.

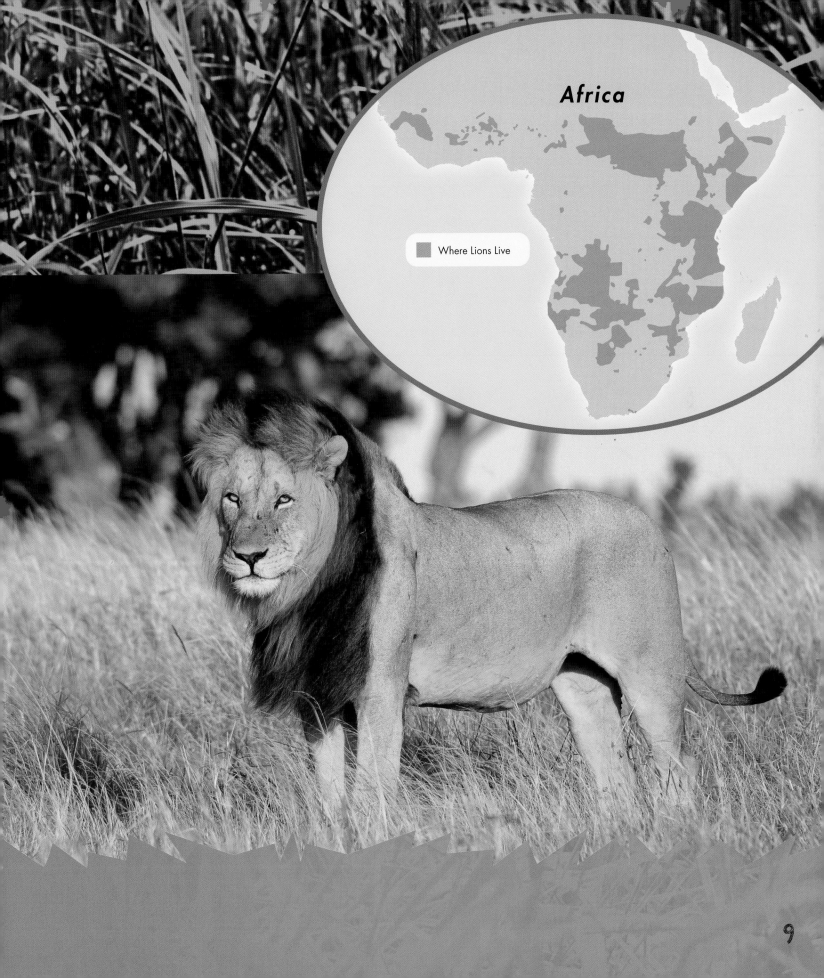

Africa

Where Lions Live

Born to hunt

Lions are carnivores. They hunt and kill other animals for food. Lions also steal food from other predators.

Hungry lions hunt large prey such as antelope and zebras. They hunt smaller prey when food is hard to find.

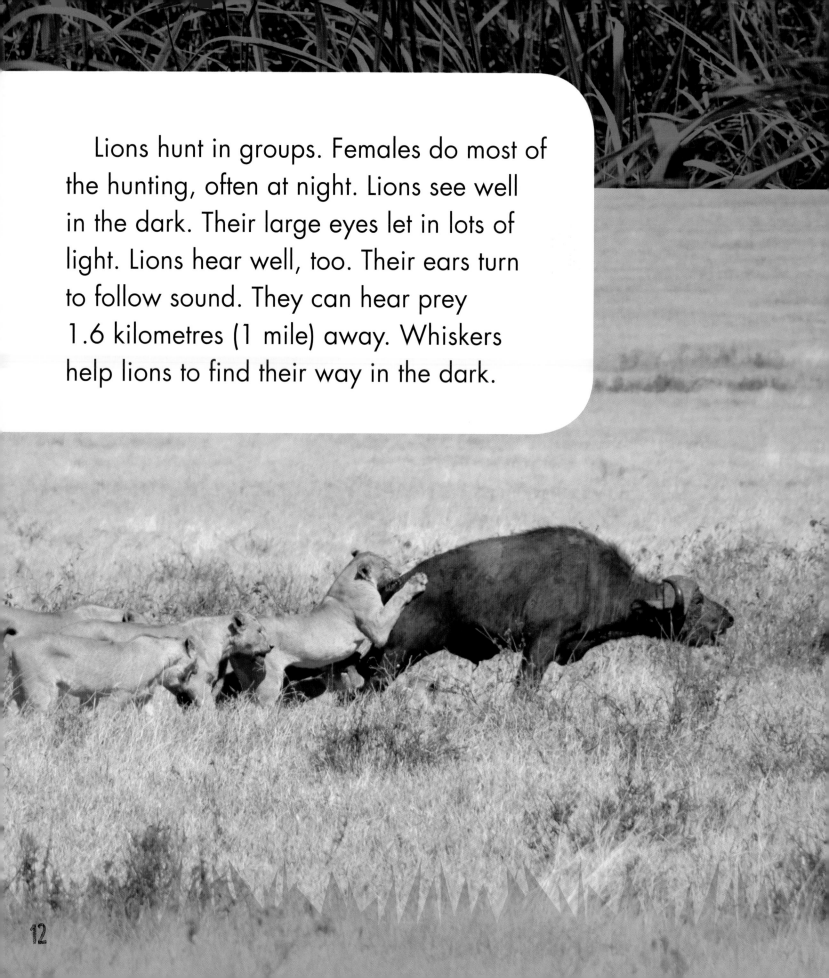

Lions hunt in groups. Females do most of the hunting, often at night. Lions see well in the dark. Their large eyes let in lots of light. Lions hear well, too. Their ears turn to follow sound. They can hear prey 1.6 kilometres (1 mile) away. Whiskers help lions to find their way in the dark.

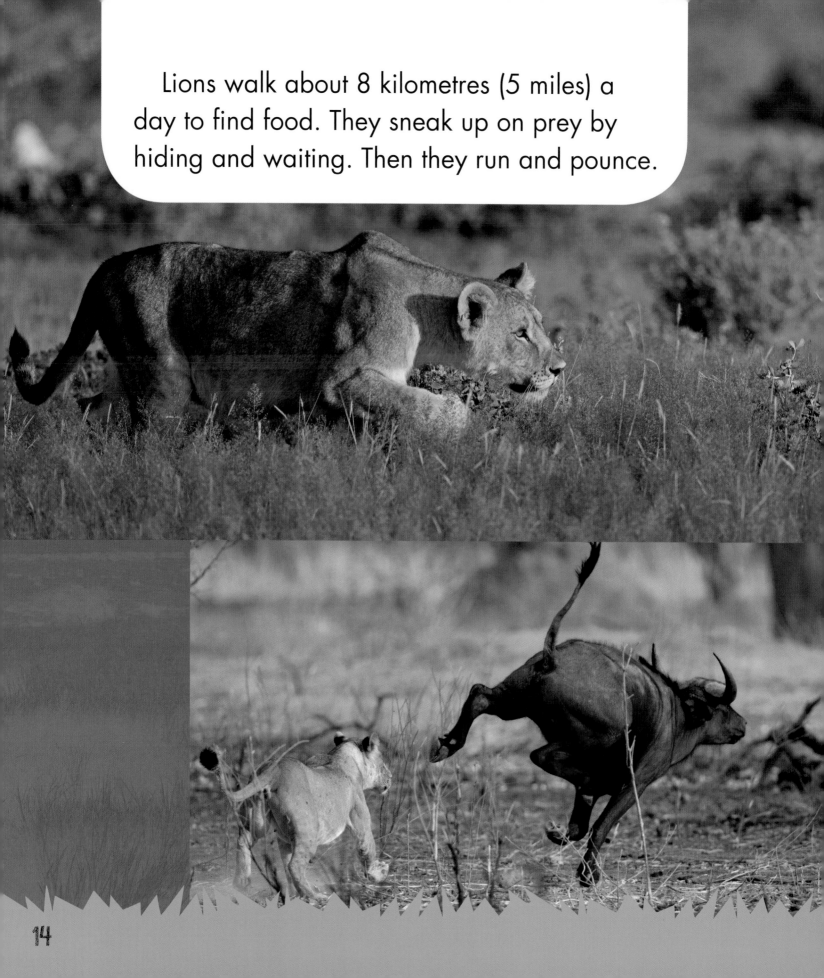

Lions walk about 8 kilometres (5 miles) a day to find food. They sneak up on prey by hiding and waiting. Then they run and pounce.

A lion can eat up to
34 kilograms (75 pounds)
of meat in one day. Then
it may not eat again for
a week.

Lions scratch
trees with their
claws. This keeps
the claws sharp. Then
they pull the claws
back into their paws.

When a lion hunts, its front claws grab the prey. Its hind claws dig into the ground.

A lion's 30 sharp teeth tear
meat from its prey. Lions have no
flat teeth for chewing. This means
they gulp down chunks of meat.

Even a lion's tongue is made for eating meat. It is rough like sandpaper. Spiny bumps cover the surface. They scrape meat from bones.

Lion families

A pride is a family of lions. Between 10 and 20 lions form a pride. Only a few are adult males. The rest are females and their young. They hunt together and share food.

The females care for all of the cubs. Males guard the territory where the pride lives and hunts. They mark this area with scent.

A female lion finds a mate when she is 3 years old. Soon, one to six cubs are born. Each tiny cub weighs about 1.4 kilograms (3 pounds). The cubs are blind for the first few days. Their mother leaves them while she goes to find food. The cubs' spots hide them in the tall grass.

Cubs stay close to their mother for about two years. She feeds them milk at first. Soon they start eating meat.

The cubs like to play. Playing together makes them strong and teaches them how to hunt.

Staying safe

Adult lions are too big for other animals to kill. Still they face many dangers. Diseases kill some lions. Leopards and hyenas can eat cubs.

Humans kill lions to protect their cattle or for sport. People also cut down trees and build homes where lions live. Then food becomes hard for the lions to find.

In some areas where lions live, people have made parks called reserves. There, no one can kill the lions. Fences keep lions from killing cattle or people. Tourists pay to see them in these reserves. With help from humans, this awesome "king of the beasts" will always rule the land.

Glossary

carnivore animal that eats only meat

cub young lion

habitat natural place and conditions in which a plant or animal lives

mane long, thick hair that grows on the head and neck of some animals such as lions and horses

plains large, flat area of land with few trees

predator animal that hunts other animals for food

prey animal hunted by another animal for food

pride group of lions living together

reserve land that is protected so that animals can live there safely

territory land on which an animal grazes or hunts for food, and raises its young

Books

Animals that Hunt (Adapted to Survive), Angela Royston (Raintree, 2014)

Mighty Lions (Walk on the Wild Side), Charlotte Guillain (Raintree, 2014)

Websites

www.bbc.co.uk/bigcat/animals/lions
Meet the Top Cats! Find out more, see photos and watch videos of this awesome pride of lions!

http://ngkids.co.uk/did-you-know/10-lion-facts
Find out more amazing lion facts and follow the links to make your own mighty lion!

Comprehension questions

1. On page 29, the text says the lion is a "king of the beasts." What do you think this name means?

2. Look at all the pictures of lions hunting throughout the book. Would a lion without teeth and claws be a good hunter? Why or why not?

3. Describe how a lion's fur keeps it hidden.

Index